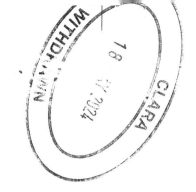

KT-373-716

Joanne Trattoria
COOKBOOK

Classic Recipes and Scenes from an Italian-American Restaurant

Joe Germanotta
with Wenonah Hoye

A POST HILL PRESS BOOK

Joanne Trattoria Cookbook:
Classic Recipes and Scenes from an Italian-American Restaurant
© 2016 by Joseph Germanotta with Wenonah Hoye
All Rights Reserved

ISBN: 978-1-68261-258-3
ISBN (eBook): 978-1-68261-259-0

Thanks to Alex Dolan, who provided many of the photos in this book. We couldn't have done it without you! [Photos: page vii; p. 3; p. 8; p. 12; p. 14; p. 20 (top); p. 27; p. 49; p. 85 (both); p. 86; p. 93]

Thanks to Bethany Michaela Jones/Sojourner Society, who shot many great photographs just for this book.

Interior Design and Composition: Greg Johnson/Textbook Perfect

Post Hill
PRESS
Post Hill Press
posthillpress.com

Published in the United States of America
3 4 5 6 7 8 9 10

This book is dedicated to my sister,
Joanne Stefani Germanotta.
Though her flame died out too early,
her light shines on
through my daughters,
Natali Veronica and Stefani Joanne.

Contents

Joe with daughters Natali and Stefani.

Foreword

Since my sister, Natali, and I were little girls, my mother and father made sure the kitchen was the centerpiece of our household. We had dinner as a family every night and ate delicious Italian-style meals that were made with love from recipes that had been passed down for generations on both sides of my family. Recipes from ancestors in Naso—a town in the Messina Province in Sicily—Santa Lucia and Venice live on through my family, each with its own distinct twist in flavor. The uniqueness of this cookbook and our family restaurant, Joanne Trattoria, lies in the influence of the immigration of our families from Italy through Ellis Island to New Jersey (where my father was raised) and West Virginia (where my mother was raised.)

The smell, every Sunday, of a pot of fresh "gravy," as we would call it instead of "tomato sauce," is one of the fondest memories I have from my childhood. I recall the smell of roasting sausages as they were dropped delicately into a slowly simmering 9–12 hour sauce. I remember the smile as my butter knife snapped open the outer layer and the juices filled my plate, sopped up by fresh pasta and followed by a crispy chopped salad made by my mother. Red wine that my father and grandfather Giuseppe made in our laundry room in the basement, sifted through cheesecloth as it was poured for everyone at the table.

We would say a prayer and then eat as a family. We ended each prayer in memory of my father's sister, Joanne, whose name has become the symbol both of our family's majestic accomplishments and of our losses along the way. We always knew there was a plate at the table missing, and we ask that when you prepare these traditional family dishes you honor the memory of those you love and those you've lost, and cook with the intention of strengthening the bonds of family and friendship in the place us Italians think is best: The Kitchen.

Love, Stefani Joanne Germanotta

Where Everybody Knows Your Name...

When my daughters were young I had my own business and I worked from home. For years, I'd be up every morning at 5:00 a.m. My wife, Cynthia, and I would get the girls off to school, we'd work all day, and then at around 4:30 meet up with a group of friends somewhere in the neighborhood to share a few drinks and some laughs. We did this religiously, every afternoon, for years. It was a nice way to unwind from the day. Around 6:00 p.m., or so, I'd head home to cook dinner for my family.

The group of us started out like nomads. We'd settle into place after place only to have it close down without warning, and force us out on the move again. Eventually, on a quiet, tree-lined street just off of Central Park, we discovered this great little restaurant on the ground floor of a hundred-year-old townhouse. It was warm and friendly, with wood-burning fireplaces, a cozy patio in the back and a bar facing the street. It was instantly welcoming. Our little group swelled to maybe a dozen or so and we became regulars, or "Irregulars" as we liked to call ourselves.

Then one evening, at our usual time, I arrived at 70 West 68th Street to find the lights out and yellow city marshal tape across the door. We'd been gathering there daily for five years, but just like that our beloved local watering hole was gone. Not long after, out of the blue, the landlord contacted me and asked if I had any interest in taking over the restaurant space.

Ever since I was a little kid, hanging around my mother's kitchen, scribbling drawings into her cookbooks while she prepared our family meals, I have dreamed of opening my own restaurant. I had graduated from Michigan State with a degree in Hospitality and Hotel Management, but took a job right out of school with a public accounting firm and never made it back to the field I loved. Now,

here I was, semi-retired, my daughters grown, presented with an opportunity that could bring my life full circle.

Cynthia and I did a walkthrough of the space with our daughters. We asked them what they thought about us taking on the challenge of opening our own restaurant, and without hesitation they said, "Let's do it!" From there, it was a whirlwind family project. We spent eight months gutting/renovating the restaurant, restoring the space to its former glory. We teamed up with Art Smith, former personal chef to Oprah Winfrey, who was instrumental in developing the menu, and in helping us get the restaurant up and running.

When Joanne Trattoria—named in honor of my sister who died of lupus at nineteen—opened its doors in February of 2012 it was the realization of my childhood dream. We are more than a neighborhood restaurant; we are a family. Most of the staff have been with us from the very beginning; my wife, Cynthia, did all the decorating; my younger daughter, Natali, has worked at the restaurant as a bartender and hostess; and my older daughter, Stefani (known to millions as Lady Gaga), has been known to stop in from time to time and when she does she always ends up behind the bar—though we usually have a mess on our hands.

Every dish we serve is personal in some way—either as a Germanotta family recipe or one that is significant to a member of the extended Joanne family. This book of our favorite recipes and stories is our gift to you.

Mangia!

~*Joe Germanotta*
Owner, Joanne Trattoria

Chapter 1

Gravy

My sister and I grew up in Elizabeth, New Jersey. For most of my early childhood our mother, Angelina Germanotta, was a stay-at-home mom who cooked dinner for us every night. She'd make mostly Italian meals: meatballs, marinara, stuffed clams, pasta fagioli, stuffed artichokes, and stuffed mushrooms. Sundays were always set aside for family and she would spend the entire day preparing a big meal. In the afternoons, while she was cooking or baking, I would sit at the kitchen table and, to keep me occupied, she would let me draw in her cookbooks.

When I was in junior high, my mother went to work with my father at our family's lawn and garden store. He had bought the shop because he was tired of working his whole life for other people; finally, he was his own boss. This was around the same time that Joanne came down with lupus. She used to get itchy bumps on her fingers, arthritis, and fatigue, but at the time we didn't really know what it was. Once my mother started working at the shop, she would call home in the afternoons to check on me and I would say, "I'm cooking"—I'm sure having her teenage son loose in her kitchen probably frightened her to death. I would make things from memory, having watched my mother in the kitchen my whole childhood. I have always loved to cook. When I finished high school, I wrote my senior paper on owning a restaurant. It was called "Feeding the People." To this day, that is my guiding principal. When Stefani is in town we'll put together a care package from the restaurant and send it over to her apartment. When I visit my mother, I always take her at least a dozen items to freeze.

Where I come from, and in other parts of the country, Italian-Americans use the word "gravy" to refer to that big pot of bubbling sauce that simmers for hours on the stove every Sunday. To us, Sunday Gravy is more than just a meal, it is a way of life; the long, slow simmering ensures that families spend time together and reinforces the bonds the keep us together. When we began preparing the menu at Joanne I wanted that spirit of family, food and love to be at the heart of every dish we serve, so I returned to my childhood memories of Sunday Gravy and looked to my mother's recipes for inspiration.

~Joe Germanotta

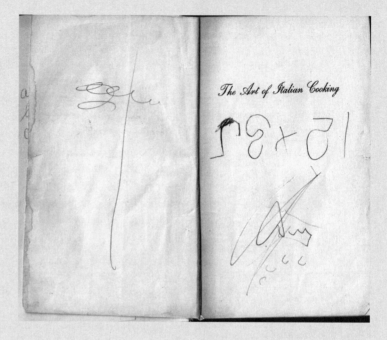

Joanne's Marinara

Made from just a handful of ingredients, marinara is a staple in Italian-American cooking. Once you have mastered the basic marinara, you can build on that recipe to make dozens of other dishes.

Juan Castillo, Kitchen Manager, making up a fresh batch of Joanne's Marinara.

Serves: 6–8

Ingredients

1 large Vidalia onion, diced
6 cloves garlic, chopped
3–4 pounds puréed San Marzano tomatoes
1 bunch basil leaves
2 tbsp. extra virgin olive oil

1. Heat olive oil in a large Dutch oven or saucepot over medium heat.
2. Add diced onion and garlic. Sauté until onions are translucent and garlic is aromatic.
3. Add basil leaves and puréed tomatoes.
4. Simmer on low for 3–4 hours—this will neutralize acidity of tomatoes, reduce water content, and bring out the sweetness of the tomatoes.
5. Serve with your choice of fresh pasta or store to use with other recipes.

Note: For the Lasagna de la Casa you will need to set aside 4–6 cups of marinara and for the Eggplant Parmesan you will need to set aside 4 cups. The preferred method for storing sauce is to can it using mason jars with lids and airtight seals, which preserves the flavor best. For this method you will need a pressure canner, which can be purchased online or from any kitchen supply store. However, you can also store it in your freezer in freezer-proof containers. To thaw, place in refrigerator overnight or place in sink with warm water and submerge the container until it's thoroughly defrosted.

Joanne's Bolognese

A rich and hearty meat-based sauce, Bolognese is Italian-American comfort food. It originates from Bologna (hence the name) in Northern Italy, where it is known simply as ragù—*Italian for meat sauce—and is classically paired with tagliatelle. At Joanne, our Bolognese is made from equal parts ground beef, veal and pork, and a thick slice of seared pancetta for added flavor. It can be served immediately over flat, broad noodles or stored for later use.*

Serves: 6–8

Ingredients

1 large carrot	1 lb. ground veal
1 large onion	1 lb. ground pork
1 large bunch celery	7 oz. tomato paste
5 cloves garlic	1½ quart can crushed tomatoes
1½-inch thick slice of pancetta	¼ cup flour
1 stem rosemary	¼ cup heavy cream
1 lb. ground beef	2 tbsp. sugar

1. Purée the carrot, onion, celery and garlic in a food processor and set aside.
2. Tie a ½-inch thick slice of pancetta and a couple of sprigs of rosemary with butcher twine.
3. In a large Dutch oven or stockpot, sear off the pancetta with rosemary and olive oil. Sear it until it is browned on both sides and the fat has rendered from the pancetta. (You will want the fat from the seasoned pancetta to sauté the vegetables.)
4. Add puréed vegetables and ground meat. Cook until meat is browned all the way through. Drain off excess fat and discard.

5. Add tomato paste and crushed tomatoes. Once combined, dust the meat mixture with flour. Stir until combined, and then add the cream and sugar.
6. Remove the pancetta bundle from the pan, cut off the twine, and discard the rosemary and twine. Chop up the pancetta and add to the pan.
7. Simmer on low for 30–45 minutes.
8. Serve with your choice of fresh pasta.

Note: For the Lasagna de la Casa you will need to set aside 4–6 cups of the Bolognese.

Pork Ragù

Although recipes vary from region to region, the ragù is a staple in Italian cooking. Traditionally served over fresh pasta, this meat-based sauce must be slow-cooked until the meat is tender and the sauce is rich and flavorful. Our Pork Ragù began as a special, but it became so popular we made it a permanent fixture on the menu.

Serves: 4–8

Ingredients

2 racks of pork ribs
1 onion, diced
1 carrot, diced
1 bunch of celery, diced
14 oz. can tomato paste
8 oz. red wine
6–8 cups chicken or vegetable stock
4 cloves garlic
3 tbsp. extra virgin olive oil
Salt and pepper to taste

1. Preheat oven to 325 degrees.
2. Slice ribs into 2- or 3-rib segments—this helps them cook faster and makes it easier to pull apart once they are done and tender. Season the ribs with salt and pepper and sear in a deep baking pan with the extra virgin olive oil. Once browned on both sides, remove from pan and set aside.
3. Place diced carrot, onion, garlic, and celery into a food processor and purée until smooth. Put puréed mixture into the pan in which you seared the ribs and sauté until onions are translucent and aromatic.

4. Stir in the can of tomato paste with the vegetables, taking care it does not burn. Once the tomato paste has coated the puréed vegetables, add the red wine and deglaze the pan, getting loose all of the bits of purée from the bottom. Place ribs in the pan and add stock until all ribs are fully covered.

5. Bake at 325 degrees for about 2 hours, or until ribs are tender and falling off the bone. Remove ribs and pull apart, discarding the bones.

6. To serve, take some of the rib meat and some of the reduced sauce from the pan and heat thoroughly on the stove.

7. Add your choice of pasta, toss, and serve.

White Truffle Alfredo

Our rich and creamy Alfredo sauce is made with a delicious assortment of wild mushrooms (trumpet, oyster, crimini, baby bella) and our own homemade white truffle cream.* It can be served on its own over fresh pasta or paired with grilled chicken for added protein.

Serves: 4

Ingredients

2 cups assorted wild mushrooms
2 tbsp. olive oil
1 tbsp. white truffle cream
1 cup Parmesan cheese
2 cups heavy cream
16 oz. fresh fettuccine
1 stem fresh basil, for garnish

1. In a skillet, heat up the olive oil and sauté the mushrooms until soft.
2. Add white truffle cream, heavy cream, and Parmesan and cook until thickened.
3. Cook pasta (according to directions) until tender or *al dente*, depending on your preference.
4. Toss pasta in the skillet and coat with sauce.
5. Garnish with basil and serve in a large bowl.

*You can either make the White Truffle Cream from our recipe or purchase it premade from your local gourmet grocery store.

White Truffle Cream

2 cups mushroom caps
olive oil
⅓ cup sunflower oil
¼ cup heavy cream
2 small shavings white truffles

1. Sauté mushrooms in olive oil over medium heat.
2. Place in a food processor and add the sunflower oil, heavy cream, and the white truffle shavings.
3. Use 2 tbsp. for the Alfredo and store the rest in an airtight container or jar for up to seven days.

MAKING HOMEMADE MARINARA with a close group of friends is one of our favorite traditions. We met Joe Maniscalco and his wife Francine at the Columbus Citizens Foundation ten years ago. Since then, we have been getting together at the end of every summer in the backyard of their home on Long Island to make sauce from fresh, locally grown plum tomatoes.

We always begin the day with a champagne toast to good food and old friends. Working from an old Sicilian recipe, we wash, boil and drain the tomatoes. While they're cooling, we chop the onions and garlic. Then we clean and separate the basil, and set it out to dry. Fina, Fran's mother who lives across the street, always stops by to check on us. Once the tomatoes have cooled, we grind them by hand, to separate the skins and make a purée. Then we combine all the ingredients and cook it all up in huge cauldrons. We work from dawn till dusk, and make enough sauce to fill over two hundred jars.

It's a long, labor intensive day, but there's always plenty of laughter and good wine to get us through the usually unbearable late August heat, and our hard work is rewarded at the end of the day with a delicious meal under the stars, enjoyed in the company of dear friends.
~Cynthia Germanotta

OPENING NIGHT WAS A MESS. We had a brand new kitchen staff, a brand new wait staff, and a packed dining room that was filled with press, well-known food critics from national newspapers, celebrities, and high profile individuals from New York City. The dishes were coming out of the kitchen too slowly; servers were getting table numbers mixed up. Everything that could go wrong went wrong. The press crucified me. On top of everything else, we had a sump pump break down that night. At one point, I went downstairs to find Chef Art Smith ankle deep in water in the basement. It was trial by fire… and water. ~*Joe Germanotta*

TRAVIS JONES, OUR GENERAL Manager and Executive Chef, grew up in Licking, Missouri. He served in the United States Navy for nine years and then went on to study Culinary Arts at Johnson and Wales. A few weeks after we opened, Chef Art brought him in to take over the day-to-day management of the restaurant and he's been with us ever since. I've basically given him the keys to the car. Travis is the backbone of Joanne Trattoria; many of the recipes on our menu, like our Pork Ragù, are his. We keep a photo of him in his Navy uniform on our family wall. ~*Joe Germanotta*

I SERVED IN THE NAVY FROM 1999 to 2008, when I was Honorably Discharged at the end of my last enlistment as a Fire Controlman First Class Petty Officer, Surface Warfare Qualified (SW). I served on board *USS Tarawa* (LHA-1) and *USS Simpson* (FFG-56), which was recently decommissioned and was the last modern US Navy warship to sink an enemy vessel in action. I graduated Cum Laude with an Associate Degree in Culinary Arts in 2011.

After interning for Chef Art, I took over as General Manager at Joanne in 2012. Because I was so busy running the restaurant, I didn't have time to go back to school and finish up my last two trimesters to graduate, but I will finally earn my Bachelor of Science degree in Culinary Arts and Food Service Management at the end of 2016. I also did a concentration in Psychology. I've always been fascinated by the way people's minds work. Having a basic understanding of Psychology comes in very handy in the food service industry.

~*Travis Jones*

(From left to right) Moises Quishpi, Lead Line Cook; Juan Castillo, Kitchen Manager; Travis Jones, Executive Chef, General Manager; Carlos Quishpi; Luis Quishpi.

WHEN HURRICANE SANDY HIT New York City in 2012, we had no staff show up for days. It was just me and Joe in the kitchen, Natali was waiting tables, and Cynthia was hosting. It was truly a family-run restaurant! I still remember Joe looking at me at the end of that first night—when we had cranked out food for more than 150 hungry people who had no power or water—and saying, "I didn't know you knew how to cook!" I looked at him puzzled, but then it dawned on me that he didn't know I already had my Associate Degree in Culinary Arts, he thought I was just going for my Bachelor's degree in Food Service Management.

That's when I took over as Executive Chef. My first order of business was hiring good kitchen staff. It took a while and we went through a few head line cooks, but eventually with the help of Juan Castillo, my Kitchen Manager, we put together a great staff. We have a family of Ecuadorian brothers, Carlos, Luis, and Moises Quishpi working for us as line cooks. We call them "The Three Quishpis." Their fourth brother, Segundo, is in Ecuador but whenever he comes back he has a job here as well.

Much like it was with the ship-mates I served with in the Navy, restaurant family *is* family.

~Travis Jones

Chapter 2

Antipasti

Joe's father was very handy. He built himself a bar in the den of their home. It was his favorite room in the house and a gathering place for the family, especially around the holidays. We would all come together before dinner to have a drink at the bar and chat while snacking on Angelina's homemade stuffed mushrooms or her famous artichoke dip. Behind the bar, his father had built these beautiful wooden cabinets with brightly colored stained glass panels in the doors. He even made a plaque for himself that hung over the bar for years. It read: *Joe's Bar*.

When his mother's eyesight began to fail and his parents moved from their family home to a condo, Joe salvaged a piece of the stained glass panels from the cabinets and the plaque that hung above his father's bar. Today that plaque hangs proudly over the bar here at Joanne and the stained glass panel adorns the mantel of the fireplace. Sadly, Giuseppe "Joseph" Anthony Germanotta passed away in 2010, but we honor his memory with the traditions of family, food, and laughter that were such a cherished part of his life.

~Cynthia Germanotta

Joanne's Meatballs

Perhaps more than any other dish, meatballs most perfectly capture the essence of Italian-American cooking. The meatball first came to the United States in the late 19ᵗʰ century by formerly impoverished Italian immigrants who for the first time found fresh meat readily available. Here at Joanne, we make hundreds of meatballs every week. Made from ground beef, pork, and veal, they can be served on their own as an appetizer topped with marinara or paired with homemade pasta.

Serves: 6–8 (makes 20 meatballs)

Ingredients

1 lb. ground beef	2 cups bread crumbs
1 lb. ground veal	4 eggs
1 lb. ground pork	2 cups Parmesan cheese
8 garlic cloves, crushed	1 bunch basil
1 bunch parsley, finely chopped	Salt and pepper to taste

1. Preheat oven to 350 degrees.
2. Cover a 9- by 13-inch baking sheet with foil and spray lightly with oil.
3. In a stand mixer or large bowl, combine garlic, parsley, beef, veal, and pork.
4. Stir in breadcrumbs, eggs, cheese, basil, salt and pepper and mix well.
5. Shape mixture into balls 1½ inches in diameter and arrange an inch apart on baking sheet.
6. Bake until golden brown and cooked through, about 15–20 minutes.
7. Serve with fresh pasta and Joanne's Marinara.

Spinach Artichoke Dip

A perennial crowd pleaser, Spinach Artichoke Dip is the perfect dish to serve at a gathering of friends and family. It's quick and easy to prepare, it doesn't require utensils, and no one can resist dipping a piece of toasted bread into its creamy, cheesy goodness.

Serves: 4

Ingredients
2 cups butter
2 cups flour
2 lb. bag chopped spinach
1 large white onion, puréed
12 cloves garlic
3 qts. heavy cream
1 can artichoke hearts, quartered
3 cups Parmesan cheese
Toasted bread

Tip: Use day-old bread to make crisp, delicious toasts to pair with this dip.

1. Make a roux with butter and flour: melt butter in a saucepan over medium heat, whisk in the flour and cook down until a thick paste forms.
2. As the roux becomes slightly brown and it begins to peel away from the edges of the pan, add the heavy cream.
3. Stir until it thickens a bit and add Parmesan cheese.
4. Purée onions and garlic in a food processor and then sauté with the spinach.
5. Slowly add the spinach and onion mixture to the roux.
6. Stir in Parmesan cheese and artichokes.
7. Serve at room temperature, with toasted bread.
8. Preheat oven to 450 degrees.
9. Slice bread and spread out on a medium-sized sheet pan. Toast for 5–7 minutes.

Arancini

With origins dating back to 10th-century Sicily, where under Arab rule balls of saffron-infused rice were said to have been served at banquet tables, today Arancini are sold throughout Southern Italy, often by street vendors from carts or frying kiosks. The name, which means little oranges, was likely inspired by the shape, size and golden color of these deep fried risotto rice balls. They come in many varieties of fillings, such as meat sauce, prosciutto, peas, and mozzarella. Our crispy Arancini, made with Arborio rice and stuffed with flavorful Mediterranean olives, have that perfect blend of crispy outer shell and creamy savory filling.

Serves: 4 (makes one dozen balls)

Ingredients

16 oz. box Arborio rice
½ cup peas
1 pinch saffron
4 cups chicken or vegetable stock
1 cup assorted olives (Mediterranean blend)
2 tbsp. salt
1 medium onion, diced
2 tbsp. extra virgin olive oil
4 egg yolks
2 cups grated Parmesan cheese
2 cups breadcrumbs

1. Place the oil in a saucepan and heat. Add chopped onions and sauté until they are translucent.
2. Stir in the Arborio rice and toss, coating with the oil and making sure it doesn't stick to the pan. Once the rice is thoroughly coated, add salt and saffron. Gradually mix in the stock, only adding more liquid as the mixture reduces down.

3. Once the rice is tender (usually about 30–40 minutes depending on the brand), remove from heat and add peas and Parmesan, stirring to combine. Then add egg yolks one at a time, stirring constantly to ensure they don't separate as they cook. Once all the ingredients are thoroughly combined, you should end up with a risotto-like mixture that is slightly thicker in consistency.
4. Spread the mixture out on a sheet pan and place in the refrigerator until it's cool enough to handle.
5. As you form balls out of the rice mixture, place a dimple in the middle. Stuff two or three mixed olives inside and close the ball around them.
6. Once all the rice balls are formed, roll each one in the breadcrumbs until thoroughly coated.
7. If you have a deep fryer, heat to 350 degrees (or heat two inches of oil in a skillet or Dutch oven). Place balls two or three at a time into the hot oil and cook until golden brown and hot all the way through. Serve with shaved Grana Padana Parmesan cheese.

Joanne's Baked Stuffed Mushrooms

These delicious stuffed mushrooms, made from Grandma Angie's recipe, are the perfect family appetizer.

Makes: 30–50 mushrooms, depending on their size.

Ingredients

2 tbsp. extra virgin olive oil
1 white onion, diced
¼ cup basil, chopped
4 oz. canned pimiento, chopped
40–50 medium mushrooms, stems removed and reserved
4–6 oz. white wine*
1 egg
½ cup Parmesan cheese, grated
⅓ of a loaf of rustic or day-old bread, cut into small, 1-inch cubes
1 cup chicken stock
Salt and pepper to taste

1. Preheat oven to 350 degrees.
2. Wipe mushrooms with a moist napkin to get as much ground material from the caps as possible. Keep stems to the side, for use in the filling—nothing goes to waste!
3. Shallow fry (partially submerge in oil) the mushrooms to soften them up so they are easier to bake and won't burn the filling.
4. Place partially cooked mushrooms on a rack to allow the excess oil to drain.
5. In a sauté pan add olive oil and onions, sauté until onions are translucent.

6. Add in the pimiento, and mushroom stems. Toss and cook for about 2 minutes, then add the white wine and bread. Toss thoroughly and ensure the liquid is absorbing into the bread. Cook until the bread is fully soaked.

7. Remove from heat.

8. In a food processor blend the ingredients from the pan, the eggs, and Parmesan cheese until fully combined. You can add more bread as needed.

9. Take the mushrooms caps and align them in rows on a sheet pan.

10. Fill a large pastry bag with the mixture and fill each mushroom cap completely. (If you do not have a pastry bag on hand, carefully spoon the mixture into the mushrooms.)

11. Bake until the tops are golden brown—add chicken stock to the bottom of the pan to keep the mushrooms moist while baking.

12. Serve hot and top with Parmesan cheese.

* The kind of bread you use will determine how much liquid you will need. If the bread is dry and stale, it will need more liquid to absorb into it to achieve the desired result. At Joanne, we use rustic semolina loaves, but you can use any type of bread—day-old is the best.

Remembrances & Musings

JUAN CASTILLO IS ONE OF THE most dedicated professionals I have ever met. He is Travis's go-to guy in the kitchen. Juan always says, "Work is work." He will do any job that needs doing around the restaurant. He's here at 9:30 in the morning every single day; you can set your clock by it. He does all the prep work for the kitchen. He'll make two hundred meatballs in a day. We calculated once that from the beginning of January to the end of May he made more than three thousand meatballs. Juan moved to the US with his wife, Crucita, from the Dominican Republic in 1979. For years he worked and lived down in Little Italy. Ana Coste, our bartender, is his niece. When we were hiring kitchen staff, she brought him to us and he has become an essential part of the Joanne family.

~Joe Germanotta

I MAKE AT LEAST SIXTY POUNDS of meatballs a week. I'll come in on Tuesday and make a couple hundred meatballs. They'll be gone by dinner the next night and I'll come back on Thursday and make another batch. For the weekend we sell twice as many meatballs, so I'm back here making meatballs on Friday and Saturday. I like to kid around with Joe that I should charge him twenty-five cents a meatball.

~Juan Castillo

GRANDMA RONNIE

TRAVIS IS MORE THAN JUST the Executive Chef at Joanne. He is family. We are very close. We shared an apartment while I was in college. We all love him. When my mom's mom came to the restaurant for the first time, she and Travis hit it off right away. Grandma Ronnie loves her wine, she loves laughter, and she loves her family. At the end of her visit Travis told her, "Ronnie, we're going to designate you your own stool." He had a special plaque made and the next time she came he presented her with her own stool.

~Natali Germanotta

NATALI AND I LIVED TOGETHER for about three years. We also lived with Stefani for a little while until she got her own place. Natali is like my sister. I'm very protective of her. I can tell her anything; we can laugh and eat donut ice cream sandwiches on the couch in the living room at 2:00 a.m. and not judge each other. Living with the Germanotta girls was amazing. We talked about food and what they liked to eat growing up. It helped me get a feel for their Italian family cooking, which helped guide me in the early days when we were still building our menu. I was also lucky enough to have access to the Germanotta and Bissett family recipes and to work with Papa Joe to create the menu we have today.

When our lease ended, Natali and her boyfriend, Alex, moved in together and—since I'm in my thirties and should be an adult by now—I decided it was time to get my own place. I met my fiancé, Irving Gonzales, in October of 2013. Our first date was for hot tea at Whole Foods in Columbus Circle. We got engaged in April 2016 and are in the process of planning our wedding. We have a Maltese named Milo and a parrot named Cracker.

~*Travis Jones*

Above: *Travis Jones, with fiancé Irving Gonzales.*
Below: *Travis Jones, with Milo and Cracker.*

WHEN WE TOOK OVER THE space we did a major renovation. All the original brick had been painted red and had to be stripped. Joe painstakingly restored the fireplaces himself. We opened up the kitchen to make it more inviting. During the renovation, we discovered that beneath the sheet rock, the walls in the private dining room were brick so we had those restored as well. I did all the decorating. I wanted the place to have an intimate, homey feel.

~Cynthia Germanotta

A FEW MONTHS AFTER WE opened, a patron came in who knew the family name Germanotta from when Joe was growing up on Linden Avenue in Elizabeth. He had brought his girlfriend from the town of Linden, New Jersey, to propose to her in front of the fireplace. He was so overjoyed, he was handing out fifty-dollar bills to all the staff. Some weeks later he came back to the restaurant and presented a commemorative plate to Joe from the mayor of Elizabeth. It now hangs with pride on our wall, alongside a portrait of Joanne, photos of Joseph and Angie Germanotta, and Cynthia's mother and father, Veronica and Paul Bissett.

~Travis Jones

Chapter 3

Entrées

My sister Joanne was a smart and talented young woman. She was studying Journalism at Penn State, but she died of lupus during her sophomore year. She was at home for several months, but it finally got to be too much and she was transferred to the hospital. They tried many different treatments, but she passed away on December 18, 1974.

Both our daughters are artists and they always felt as though their creativity was channeled through their aunt. From her very first tour, Stefani began the tradition of a family prayer with all the dancers and everybody that worked onstage and behind the scenes. Just before she went onstage, they would gather in a big circle and put hands together in the center. Stefani would shout, "Joanne" as they raised their hands. They did this for every single one of the 284 shows during that tour. It's a tradition that continues to this day.

Even though they were grieving the loss of their daughter, my parents still encouraged me to go away for college. So I went off to Michigan State to pursue my dream of owning my own restaurant. I lived in the dorm for the first few years, but when I moved off campus I would cook for my roommates every night from my mother's recipes for lasagna, baked pork chops, chicken—things we could afford.

Cynthia and I have been married for thirty-three years. We met when we were in our twenties, back when we both worked for companies in software solutions. She was in sales and I was developing software applications that would manage inventory, sales, databases and financial analysis tools. In my office we had a nightline, so when someone called in after six o'clock, everyone's phone would ring and whoever was free would pick up. Often I would answer the phone and it would be Cynthia calling for her friend, who worked in sales in my office. If she was busy, I would strike up a conversation with Cynthia and we got to be friendly. We had never met, but we would chat and she would tell me about her boyfriend—I thought he sounded like a handful.

This went on for months. Then one night my roommate and I were out having cocktails and I got to chatting with this beautiful blonde at the bar. After a while, she mentioned her friend Karen. I said, "Hang on. Are you Cynthia? I'm Joe!"

It was destiny.

~Joe Germanotta

Lemon Artichoke Chicken

Made from Grandma Angie's recipe, this take on the classic Chicken Piccata makes use of artichoke hearts instead of capers. Like the Piccata, it's a simple recipe that is quick and easy to make—great for whipping up on a weeknight or, paired with a salad and a nice glass of wine, can be perfect for those last-minute dinner guests.

Serves: 4

Ingredients

4–8 oz. chicken breasts, sliced in half lengthwise
8 artichoke hearts, sliced into quarters
¼ cup lemon juice
2 cups chicken stock
2 tbsp. butter
2 tbsp. extra virgin olive oil
1 cup flour, for dredging
Salt and pepper to taste

1. In a large bowl, combine the flour, salt, and pepper. Dredge the sliced chicken in the flour and set aside.
2. Heat olive oil in a large skillet and carefully place the chicken breast pieces into the pan.
3. When chicken is cooked thoroughly on both sides, 3 to 4 minutes per side, add artichoke hearts, lemon juice, chicken stock and butter to the pan. Simmer until the liquid reduces down and becomes slightly thickened—the sauce will coat the back of your spoon.
4. Adjust the flavor with salt or pepper to taste.
5. To serve, place two pieces of chicken breast on a dish and top with the sauce and artichoke hearts. Or toss your favorite pasta in the leftover sauce from the pan after the chicken has been removed.

Papa G's Chicken

Chicken Scarpariello is a classic Italian-American dish that is a perfect combination of flavor and culture. It is traditionally rustic fare, made from hearty, affordable ingredients. In fact, scarpariello means shoemaker in Italian, and the story goes that it got its name because even a shoemaker could afford it. Despite its humble name, this dish has a rich and robust flavor. We've got it on the menu as Papa G's Chicken and it is our most popular dish.

Servings: 4–6

Ingredients

2–2½ lbs. white (organic) chicken
    (cut pieces on the bone,
    2 from the leg/thigh,
    2 from the breast and
    1 from the wing joint)
6 sweet Italian sausage links, sliced
24 pepperoncini peppers, with juice
8 garlic cloves, sliced
1 tbsp. dried oregano leaves
1 cup red wine vinegar
1 tbsp. parsley, chopped
¼ cup olive oil
Black pepper, to taste

1. Fry the chicken pieces for 8 minutes in a deep fryer heated to 350 degrees (or in a large skillet or Dutch oven with 2 inches of oil over medium-high heat.)

2. In a sauté pan heat the olive oil over medium heat and then add the garlic, sausage and oregano.

3. When the garlic is browned and the sausage is brown and crispy on both sides, add the chicken. Toss and immediately deglaze with the vinegar and pepperoncini peppers.

4. Transfer chicken and sauce to a platter, add ground black pepper to taste, and garnish with the parsley.

Eggplant Parmesan

At Joanne we make our Eggplant Parmesan to order; this keeps the eggplant light and crispy and the result is a dish that is fresh and full of flavor.

Serves: 6–8 hearty portions

Ingredients

2 large eggplants, peeled and sliced (½-inch thick)
2 cups flour for dredging
6 eggs, mixed together in a bowl
6 cups breadcrumbs
4 cups Joanne's Marinara
4–6 cups fresh mozzarella cheese, shredded
Salt and pepper to taste

1. In a bowl, whisk together eggs and set aside.
2. In separate bowl, mix the flour with salt and pepper and set aside.
3. Place breadcrumbs in a third bowl and set aside.
4. Dip the eggplant into the egg wash, then into the flour, then into egg wash again and then into the breadcrumbs. Repeat until all eggplant slices are coated in egg wash, flour, and breadcrumbs.
5. Fill a pan with just enough oil to fry the sliced eggplant. You will want to fry the eggplant until crispy and brown on both sides. (To prevent them from absorbing the oil and becoming mushy, ensure that the pan with the oil is preheated before placing eggplant.)
6. After cooking, line the slices on a rack to drain excess oil.

7. Once they have cooled, layer the bottom of a 9- by 13-inch pan with fried eggplant slices, then add a layer of marinara and Parmesan cheese, then more eggplant and another layer of sauce and cheese.
8. Top it off with marinara and mozzarella.
9. Bake in the oven at 350 degrees for 20–25 minutes or until golden brown and bubbly.

Lasagna de la Casa

One of our most popular dishes at Joanne, the Lasagna de la Casa, makes use of our Marinara as well as our Bolognese, so when making those it's wise to set aside several cups of each for use in this recipe.

Serves: 6–8 (hearty portions)

Ingredients

Joanne's Bolognese, 4–6 cups

Joanne's Marinara, 4–6 cups

4 cups ricotta cheese

1 bunch parsley, finely chopped

1 egg, separated

Parmesan cheese

4–6 cups fresh mozzarella, shredded

½–1 lb. dry lasagna noodles

1. Preheat oven to 350 degrees.
2. Spray a large 2-inch deep baking dish (9- by 13-inches wide) with nonstick cooking spray and set aside.
3. In a large bowl, mix together the ricotta, parsley, egg yolk, Parmesan cheese and stir until combined.
4. Place noodles in a large pot of boiling water and cook until tender. Remove pasta from water and put into an ice bath to cool.
5. Begin with a layer of marinara on the bottom. Then add a layer of pasta, a layer of Bolognese, another layer of pasta, then a layer of the ricotta cheese mixture, another layer of pasta and continue like so until your pan is full. Top off with a sheet of pasta, marinara and mozzarella. Bake until golden brown and bubbly, approximately 45 minutes.
6. Let stand about 10 minutes before slicing. This will allow the lasagna to firm up a bit and hold its shape, so you don't end up with a mess on your plate!

Remembrances & Musings

THE COLUMBUS CITIZENS Foundation is a nonprofit philanthropic organization dedicated to celebrating Italian-American heritage and nurturing achievement within the community. Each year the Foundation awards scholarships and grants to deserving Italian-American students, from elementary through college age. All the money raised through the parade in New York City on Columbus Day weekend, as well as all membership dues, goes to supporting these programs.

BEING MEMBERS OF THE Columbus Citizens Foundation for so many years, we've gotten to know many of the executive staff. John Boden and I, in particular, have become close over the years. We even share the same heart surgeon and when he was in the hospital a few years back, recovering from open-heart surgery, I brought him care packages from Joanne to the hospital. When I was creating the

Cynthia and family friend Kathy McGinty at the Columbus Day Parade.

menu for Joanne, I wanted to honor the Foundation, so I called John and asked him if he'd be willing to contribute a recipe to our menu. He said, "Of course," and came down to the restaurant to work with our chefs. Both my Sicilian grandfathers were shoemakers, so it seemed a fitting tribute to our family history that the recipe we settled on, Chicken Scarpariello, is named after these humble craftsmen.

~*Joe Germanotta*

I HAVE KNOWN THE
Germanottas since Joe and Cynthia
became members of the Columbus
Citizens Foundation in 2001. Joe
has sat on our scholarship board for
many years and he and Cynthia still
help to organize New York City's
landmark Annual Columbus Day
Parade. When he first bought the
restaurant, Joe asked me to come
over and work with his chefs on a
few things they could include on
the menu. Our Chicken Scarpariello
is one of the most popular dishes
at the Foundation, but we are only
open to members so I thought this
would be a great way share this
delicious dish with the general
public.

If you asked twenty different
chefs to make Chicken Scarpariello you'd get twenty very different
dishes. I've seen it made with
brown sauce and mushrooms and
I've seen it lightly glazed with
lemon wine. My interpretation,
which incorporates sweet sausage
and pepperoncini, came from
opera impresario Frank Celenza, a
respected New York prosthodontist

and author, who was an active
member of the Foundation for many
years before he passed away in
2008. Frank was able to meld his
love of gourmet food, fine wines,
and opera by hosting more than
seventy now legendary opera nights
at the Foundation. Frank and I

worked on this recipe together and
I am pleased that it has gone on to
become one of Joanne's signature
dishes.

~*John L. Boden*
General Manager, Executive Chef
Columbus Citizens Foundation

THE WAY THE RESTAURANT was built—from the menu to the decor—is not just about the food. It reflects our family history and our values. When we were doing the renovations my dad sanded every inch of the brick fireplaces himself. My mom is always coming in and decorating for the holidays. She'll come up with a theme or my sister will come up with an idea and we'll all get together and decorate. There have been times where we've done a full repaint. We'll be at the restaurant all weekend with my dad and I'll go home covered in paint.

My mom did all the decorating. As you walk in there are two maps, one of Venice and one of Sicily, to represent the areas of Italy where my grandparents came from. Just past the bar is our family wall. There's a portrait of my Aunt Joanne. There are photos of my grandparents, there's even a photo of Travis in his Navy uniform. Throughout the restaurant are antiques that came from my grandparents' home, like the antique clock that sits on the mantel that belonged to my dad's father.

~Natali Germanotta

WHEN THE GIRLS WERE growing up, we taught them how to cook. They had their own aprons and rolling pins. We made fresh pasta and taught them how. We would make the dough from scratch and roll out the noodles in a pasta machine with a hand crank. This family ritual goes back to my own mother and her sisters, who had a tradition of making homemade ravioli.

~Cynthia Germanotta

Cynthia with sister, Sheri Bissett Cates.

OWNING A RESTAURANT HAS been a dream of my dad's for as long as I can remember. Growing up, he was always making some big Italian dinner every night. Sunday meals were a very big deal in our family. My dad would usually start cooking around 1:00, as soon as we got home from Mass, but sometimes he'd even set the oven to start roasting or baking while we were at church. He'd make things like meatballs from my grandmother's recipe, lemon chicken with escarole, baked artichokes, and pasta with cherry tomatoes and pine nuts. If the weather was nice, he would do a grill feast and we would all sit out on the patio. For my dad, it was about making the food and enjoying it, but it was also about taking a long time to eat the meal and spending that time together as a family.

~Natali Germanotta

Chapter 4

Thanksgiving Dinner

Towards the end of 2011, most of the renovations were done and things at Joanne were finally falling into place. For Thanksgiving we decided to have a small dinner at the restaurant for the family and a few close friends who were in town. We weren't even open yet, but we bought linens and set up tables in the back. The girls and I decorated for the holiday. We had the fireplace going. It was really lovely.

In the end, our small dinner swelled to over thirty guests: Chef Art Smith and his husband, artist Jesus Salgueiro; our daughters and their boyfriends; some people from Stefani's tour who were in the city for the holiday; and a number of close friends and family members. Before sitting down to dinner that night, we all gathered for a drink at the bar. As we finished our cocktails and moved to the back of the restaurant to sit down to dinner, Natali remarked that it's a good luck tradition to break a plate. I looked over at Stefani, who was standing in the threshold of the dining area. She had picked up a plate and had it raised hands-over-head. I gasped as she slammed the plate down. It shattered and chipped one of our brand new floor tiles. Joe was not happy about that, but it became an unforgettable moment from a very special night that our family will always cherish. We were together with our daughters and loved ones and Joanne was our new home.

Unbeknownst to us, Jesus gathered up the pieces of the plate, which—as fate would have it—had broken in the shape of a heart. He crafted them into a beautiful piece of artwork and presented it to us some weeks later. Hearts are very meaningful symbols in Jesus's work, so it all "fell" together, so to speak.

~Cynthia Germanotta

Fried Turkey

Inspired by Chef Art's famous fried chicken, this Thanksgiving Fried Turkey is a great spin on the holiday classic.

Serves: 6

Ingredients

1 (10–12 lb.) whole turkey
1½ tbsp. each: dry sage, thyme, Italian parsley, garlic powder
1 tbsp. each: onion powder, salt and black pepper
3 gallons peanut oil, for frying

Photo of Lady Gaga and Art Smith courtesy of A Very Gaga Thanksgiving, *which aired on ABC on Thanksgiving 2011.*

1. Preheat oil to 375 degrees.
2. Remove giblets and neck from body cavities of turkey. Discard or refrigerate for another use. Pat turkey dry with paper towels to ensure less oil splatter when frying. Do not use the turkey lifter in fryer.
3. Combine all the dry ingredients and rub the turkey with them.
4. Place turkey, breast side up, in basket. Slowly lower basket into hot oil, being cautious of splattering oil. Maintain oil temperature at about 350 degrees.
5. Fry turkey for 3½ minutes per pound. (Do not open the fryer until the designated time is up.) Remove from oil to check if done. Insert an instant-read thermometer into thickest part of thigh, not touching bone. Temperature should read 180 degrees.
6. Remove the turkey and place it on a wooden board to cool.

Chef Art's Gravy

Tomato gravy is very popular throughout the South, where it is traditionally served over hot, homemade biscuits. Here, Chef Art has taken his own family recipe for gravy and combined it with Joanne's Marinara.

Makes: 4 cups of gravy

Ingredients

4 tbsp. olive oil, plus 2 tbsp.

½ cup of pancetta, chopped

1 onion, chopped fine

2 pieces of celery, chopped fine

2 cloves of garlic, minced

6 tbsp. flour

½ cup white wine, optional

4 cups turkey broth, hot

¼ cup Joanne's Marinara

¼ cup heavy cream

4 tbsp. soft butter, optional

3 tbsp. finely chopped fresh thyme

Sea salt, to taste

Fresh-ground pepper to taste

1. Sauté pancetta in a pan with olive oil until crispy. Remove from pan and set aside.
2. In the same pan, sauté onions, celery, and garlic and cook until translucent.
3. Sprinkle flour over vegetables and cook for 5 minutes over medium heat. If too dry add more oil to form a roux.
4. Add white wine and cook until liquid reduces by half.
5. Add hot broth and simmer until liquid is reduced by half. (For a finer gravy, strain to remove vegetables and return to pan.)
6. Stir in Joanne's Marinara.
7. Whisk in cream and butter. Season with thyme, salt, and fresh ground pepper to finish.

Grandma Angie's Salami Pecorino Cheese Waffles

This recipe was inspired by Angelina Germanotta's salami and pecorino Italian stuffing. Those familiar flavors have been turned into a waffle by Chef Art Smith. Enjoy them sprinkled with grated pecorino cheese, hot off the iron or top them with fried turkey or fried chicken.

Joe dancing with his mother, Angelina Germanotta.

Serves: makes 6 waffles

Ingredients

1¼ cups all purpose flour

¼ cup cornmeal, fine

2 tbsp. baking powder

1 tbsp. each freshly chopped Italian parsley,
    rosemary and thyme

¼ cup finely grated pecorino cheese
    or Italian Parmesan cheese,
    plus extra to top the waffles

½ cup thinly sliced salami,
    fried crispy, reserve 20 thinly
    sliced pieces

1¾ cups whole milk

2 eggs, beaten

6 tbsp. extra virgin olive oil

1. In a large bowl, combine flour, cornmeal, and baking powder and sift together with a whisk.
2. Add herbs and cheese and toss.
3. Fry salami in olive oil till crispy. Remove from oil and blot on towels to drain. Chop into a fine crumble. Reserve the cooking oil for batter.
4. In a second bowl, combine milk, eggs, reserved oil, and beat well.
5. Add wet ingredients to dry ingredients and mix carefully—but do not over beat. Fold in crumbled salami.
6. Preheat waffle iron and spray generously with cooking spray. Place thinly sliced, uncooked salami on waffle grates. Pour batter on grates and bake according to manufacturer's directions.
7. Bake until golden and crisp.

Chef Art's Homecoming Florida Kitchen Collard Greens

Direct from the menu at Chef Art's Homecoming Florida Kitchen, this recipe for Collard Greens is perfect for a Southern spin on the traditional Thanksgiving feast.

Serves: 6

Ingredients

½ lb. collard greens, stems removed, cleaned and chopped
½ lb. kale, stems removed, cleaned and chopped
2 tbsp. canola oil
⅛ cup apple cider vinegar
⅛ cup white wine vinegar
¼ cup diced red onion
⅓ cup diced white onion
1 tsp. garlic, minced
¼ tsp. red pepper flakes
1 tbsp. olive oil
2 tsp. sugar
1 qt. vegetable stock
Salt and pepper to taste

1. In a large saucepot over medium-high heat, heat canola oil.
2. Add diced onion and cook for 6-8 minutes, add red pepper flakes and garlic; cook for another 2 minutes.
3. Next add the vinegar, sugar, vegetable stock, and then the greens. Cover and turn the heat to low, mix every 30 minutes for 2 hours. Do not turn heat up, when tender remove from heat and serve.

Grandma Ronnie's Cranberry Sauce

Tangy and sweet, Grandma Ronnie's recipe for homemade cranberry sauce is the perfect complement to any Thanksgiving feast. To spice up the holiday, try Aunt Sheri's and Uncle Steve's Spiced Pecans. They can be crushed and added to Grandma Ronnie's Cranberry Sauce just before serving, or enjoyed as a delicious stand-alone snack.

Servings: 6

Ingredients

2 bags fresh cranberries
½ cup water
1 cup fresh orange juice
2 cups natural cane sugar
1 cup fresh orange segments
1 cup Aunt Sheri's and Uncle Steve's Spiced Pecans (optional)

1. Bring orange juice, water and cane sugar to a boil in a large saucepan over medium heat.
2. Reduce heat and add the two bags of cranberries. Slowly simmer, stirring occasionally, until the berries pop and the mixture thickens—about 10–12 minutes.
3. Remove from heat, allow to cool and fold in the orange segments.
4. Cover and chill at least two hours before serving.

Aunt Sheri's and Uncle Steve's Spiced Pecans

11.5 oz. bag of pecans
5 tbsp. unsalted butter
5 tbsp. light brown sugar
¼ tsp. cayenne pepper, optional
1 tsp. vanilla syrup (not extract)

1. On a rimmed baking sheet, spread out the pecans and bake for 10 minutes at 350 degrees.
2. Meanwhile, put all the remaining ingredients in a microwave safe bowl and heat for 45 seconds in the microwave.
3. Toss hot nuts in the sugar mixture and then spread them back out on the rimmed baking sheet to cool.
4. Before serving return to oven for 3–5 minutes. Remove and let cool. Dry thoroughly before transferring to a bowl.

Angie Germanotta's
Perfect Apple Pie

What Thanksgiving dinner would be complete without a freshly baked, homemade apple pie? For the perfect blend of tart and sweet, use either Golden Delicious, Braeburn, or Granny Smith apples.

Serves: 6

Ingredients

Filling	*Crust*
6–8 tart apples (about 6 cups)	5 cups all purpose flour
¾ to 1 cup sugar	1 tsp. salt
2 tbsp. flour	1 tsp. baking powder
½–1 tsp. cinnamon	½ cup shortening
dash ground nutmeg	1 tsp. vinegar
dash salt	1 egg
2 tbsp. butter	

1. Place apple slices in a large bowl. Stir in the dry filling ingredients and toss until apples are evenly coated. Set mixture aside.
2. For the crust, mix together flour, salt, and baking powder. Cut in shortening. The resulting mixture should be the texture of cornmeal.
3. In a one-cup measuring cup, beat together vinegar and egg. Then fill it to one cup with cold water.
4. Combine the dry and wet ingredients and form into two balls—dough will be soft and sticky.

Alex Dolan, Natali Germanotta, and Travis Jones.

5. On a well-floured board, roll out a disk of dough, roughly 12 inches in diameter. Transfer to a lightly floured, 9-inch pie plate. Roll the remaining dough into another disk and set aside.
6. Mound the apple and sugar mixture into the pie pan. Dot with 2 tbsp. butter.
7. Cover with the remaining dough and trim the edges. Chill 30–40 minutes before baking.
8. Heat oven to 425 degrees and bake for 1 hour.

Remembrances & Musings

I FIRST MET THE GERMANOTTAS when Gaga appeared on *Oprah* in early 2010. She was on tour and had just performed at the Rosemont Theater, just outside of Chicago. When I heard she was going to be on the show, I stayed up all night and cooked. I decided to make something healthy and something comforting. When she tried my fried chicken and waffles she said to Oprah, "You sent this master chef to make comfort food for me when I needed comforting." It was the first time she had tried fried chicken and waffles.

Someone from *Oprah* hooked us up with tickets, so we went to watch Gaga perform that night. My husband, Jesus, and I met Joe and Cynthia for the first time backstage. I was immediately struck by what a supportive and loving family they are. What I love most about Gaga is how close she is with her father. Joe is the greatest stage-father that ever lived. He will always protect her.

In May 2011, Gaga appeared on Oprah's last show and we had dinner with Joe and Cynthia at my restaurant, Table 52. Shortly after,

Gaga invited me to appear in a cooking segment for her television special, *A Very Gaga Thanksgiving*, which was filmed at the Convent of the Sacred Heart, her former high school on the Upper East Side. Initially I had wanted to do my fried chicken and waffles, but she said, "It's Thanksgiving; we need to do turkey." So I took her grandmother's recipe for Italian stuffing and infused my waffle recipe with crispy salami and pecorino cheese and served it with fried turkey.

~Chef Art Smith

WE MET CHEF ART THROUGH

Stefani. He's cooked for President Obama and Jeb Bush, and he was Oprah Winfrey's personal chef for years. He was instrumental in helping us get the restaurant up and running. He spent a fair amount of time here after the renovations were done, getting us organized, and hiring staff. He told us what equipment to buy and hooked us up with vendors. We couldn't have opened without him.

~ Joe Germanotta

JOE IS THE MOST GENEROUS

man I have ever met. Any time Stefani has a concert or an event, he'll always get tickets for all the staff. There have been so many times when he's paid medical bills for members of the staff, myself included. When I had a herniated disc and it was getting to the point where I couldn't even move my neck, the VA wanted to operate. Joe was skeptical about the surgery, so he sent me to his chiropractor for four months and paid for the whole thing.

~Travis Jones

AROUND THE TIME WE WERE

working on the Thanksgiving special with Gaga, Jesus and I had dinner at the Columbus Citizens Foundation. Joe mentioned he was opening a restaurant and we decided to partner up. Shortly after we opened, Joe Manganiello held his after-party for *Magic Mike* at Joanne. It was a star-studded affair. I remember late into the evening, Joe sat with me on the stoop outside the restaurant and we shared a cigar. I said to him, "You're a beautiful man, why don't you have a girlfriend?" He confided to me that he had just met a woman named Sophia and he had fallen madly in love with her. Two years later he married Sofía Vergara.

~Chef Art Smith

I WORKED AT THE RESTAURANT

the first summer after we opened. I started off as a hostess and then my dad was looking to add a bartender for brunch so I started working behind the bar as well. My boyfriend, Alex, is house photographer for private events and works here as a server. He revamped the website and takes all the photographs of the food.

All the staff at Joanne are supertalented. One of the waitresses who used to work here, Meaghan, was an opera singer, so when we'd sing happy birthday it always sounded amazing. Elise, who is a server, is one of my closest friends. She is very dear to our family. My dad treats her like she's one of his own. She's been with us almost from the beginning. She's such an inspiring person who puts action to her beliefs. She volunteers for Born This Way Foundation, which was founded by my mother and sister and focuses on youth empowerment and issues like self-confidence and anti-bullying. Elise is always the first person to volunteer when the foundation teams up with the restaurant because she is a very passionate person.

~Natali Germanotta

IN 2009 I INTERNED WITH CHEF Art Smith in Chicago at his now renovated and renamed former Table 52. I had been working while going to school at my friend's store in Newport, Rhode Island and Chef Art came in to buy a shirt for his husband, Jesus. A friend of mine immediately recognized him from *Top Chef* and *Top Chef Masters* and told him that I was going to culinary school. We got to talking and after a while he said, "I can teach anyone how to cook, but I can't teach you how to be a good person. I can tell you have a big heart. Let me know when you have an internship and you can come work for me in Chicago." When I told him that I actually had an internship coming up and hadn't found a place yet, he immediately said, "Come to Chicago. You will intern for me and stay in my house."

So I moved to Chicago and stayed in their spare room for three months. I couldn't believe my good fortune. Here I was, a newbie in culinary school, cooking for donors attending big charity dinners for Common Threads, Chef Art's charity that teaches underprivileged children about nutrition and how to cook. I prepped, I cooked, I made staff smoothies every night and I hated leaving because they became like family.

When Chef Art and Jesus got married, they asked if I would help cook for the reception, so I flew to Washington DC and fried a TON of chicken. Chef Art and Jesus truly welcomed me with open arms like a son. They took a chance on a squid who was going to culinary school and working in a shoe store part-time, all because they could tell I had a good heart.

~*Travis Jones*

MY DAD THREW A BIG DINNER for the entire staff on one of the first Thanksgivings after we opened. We got to invite everyone that was involved in getting the restaurant together. We set up tables in the back and we all sat down and had a giant family meal.

We've definitely gotten creative on Thanksgiving over the years. One year, my dad made "Chef Emeril Lagasse's Turduckin," which is a chicken, inside a duck, inside a turkey. On another Thanksgiving we made Chef Art's Fried Turkey and my sister made two Peking ducks.

~*Natali Germanotta*

Chapter 5

Salads

After dating for a little more than a year, Cynthia and I got married. We had our wedding in the small chapel at St. Patrick's Cathedral and our reception at The Plaza. In the early years, we would go out to dinner a lot because we were both working. We would meet after work at six o'clock every night and have dinner at this great Italian place on 83rd and Broadway, where they made fresh pasta. When Stefani came along a few years later, we started bringing her with us. Sal, the manager, would pick her up and parade her around the restaurant. She would charm everyone in the room.

When the girls were babies we never gave them jarred food. I would go to the butcher and get a good piece of filet, or lamb, or pork chop. I'd put the meat in a pressure cooker with carrots and celery. Then I'd grind it all up into a purée and freeze it in ice cube trays. As the girls got older and were in school, we fell into a regular routine where I would cook every night and Cynthia would help the girls with their homework and get them bathed and ready for school the next day. Then we'd all sit down together and have dinner as a family.

When I was growing up my mother always had a salad at the end of the meal. It was how she cleansed her palate. Salads are an integral part of the menu at Joanne. They can be served before or after the meal, or even as the meal itself. Cynthia loves antipasto, but she prefers to have it all chopped up in a salad. That's how we came up with the Cynthia Salad.

~Joe Germanotta

Cynthia Salad

Our most popular salad, this delicious take on the classic Italian antipasto platter is bursting with soft and nutty fontina, subtly sweet Grana Padano, crisp bell peppers, juicy tomatoes, and flavorful Kalamata and Sicilian olives.

Serves: 4

Ingredients

1 red and 1 yellow bell pepper, julienned
1 oz. can roasted pimiento, julienned
1 cup curly endive, roughly chopped
1 cup radicchio, roughly chopped
2 oz. sun dried tomatoes
2 oz. diced tomato
2 oz. jar artichoke hearts
2 oz. Grana Padano hard cheese
2 oz. fontina cheese
2 oz. Gorgonzola cheese
2 oz. mixed Mediterranean olive blend (Kalamata and Sicilian)
1 small Japanese seedless cucumber
Joanne's Vinaigrette

1. Julienne (slice in long strips) the red and yellow peppers.
2. Cube the fontina and Grana Padano.
3. Slice the cucumber and the pimentos.
4. Quarter the artichoke hearts.
5. Dice the sun dried and beefsteak tomatoes.
6. Combine all the ingredients except the olives in a large bowl.
7. Crumble in the Gorgonzola cheese and add olives whole.
8. Drizzle with Joanne's Vinaigrette and serve immediately.

Joanne's Vinaigrette

Ingredients

2 oz. white balsamic vinegar
6 oz. extra virgin olive oil
Salt and pepper to taste

Add all three ingredients into a squeeze bottle or container with a tight-fitting lid and shake to incorporate evenly.

Brussels Sprouts Salad with Lemon Vinaigrette

Raw Brussels sprouts have a surprisingly delicate and sweet, cabbage-like flavor when shaved into thin, uniform slices and paired with lemon vinaigrette. For this light and flavorful, slaw-like salad you will need either a very sharp knife and excellent cutting skills, or a multi-blade slicing tool, like a mandolin (which can be purchased from any kitchen supply store).

Serves: 4

Ingredients
Two 8 oz. packages whole Brussels sprouts
¼ cup Parmesan cheese
2 tbsp. lemon juice
4 leaves radicchio
Joanne's Vinaigrette (See page 48)

1. Very carefully, shave the Brussels sprouts using the thinnest blade on a mandolin slicer and place in a large bowl.
2. Combine the lemon juice and Joanne's Vinaigrette in a container with a tight-fitting lid and shake well. Pour the vinaigrette over the shaved sprouts and toss with the Parmesan cheese.
3. Form the radicchio leaves into the shape of a bowl. Fill with dressed Brussels sprouts and serve immediately.

Red Quinoa, Arugula, and Beet Salad

Quinoa is one of the few plant-based foods considered to be a perfect protein, meaning it has all nine essential amino acids necessary for good health. Just one cup contains 8 grams of protein, 5 grams of fiber, and 15% of the recommended DV of iron. Although it's often referred to as a grain, it's actually a seed from the beet family. It comes in a rainbow of colors and has a nutty flavor that makes it the perfect addition to any salad.

Serves: 4–6

Ingredients

1 cup quinoa, cooked
16 oz. package baby arugula or regular arugula
2 red beets, roasted and quartered
2 yellow beets, roasted and quartered
Joanne's Vinaigrette (See page 48)
4 tbsp. brown mustard

1. Rinse the arugula and set aside in a large bowl.
2. Slice the roasted beets about a quarter-inch thick, then cut each slice into quarters and set aside.
3. Prepare Joanne's Vinaigrette and add brown mustard.
4. Drizzle over the arugula, sprinkle the red quinoa over the top, and finish it with the beets.
5. Serve immediately.

Remembrances & Musings

I GREW UP IN MCMECHEN, West Virginia. We had a vegetable garden and fruit trees: apple, peach, and mulberry. We lived close to several farms and once a week the farmers would drive into town and stop on our block with their fresh goods: corn, berries, tomatoes, lettuce. We used all these and the fruits and vegetables from our garden in our family meals.

Sunday dinners were always a big deal in our families, so when Joe and I had our own children it was natural that we would continue this tradition. Every Sunday, Stefani and Natali would be at the table doing their homework, while Joe and I prepared dinner. This always took me back to fond memories of my family dinners.

~Cynthia Germanotta

Bissett family: (back) Grandma Ronnie, Grandpa Paul, Cynthia, and Sheri Cates Bissett (front) Stefani and Natali.

I WAS HIRED IN MARCH 2015. Ana, the Bar Manager, had just given birth to her son, Jameson, and they were looking for someone to take over her shifts behind the bar. I had no idea what I was walking into. Joanne is not like any other restaurant. We are a family of artists and Joe's dedication to the arts means that we work in an environment that fosters creativity and collaboration among the staff. He always asks us about and is interested in our projects, and he comes out to support all of us as much as he can.

I run a small nonprofit called Open Windows that provides support to victims of domestic violence. We do fundraisers through my theater company, Purple Ribbon Shakespeare. Most recently, we developed an immersive play called *Lucy's Sick*, loosely based on *Richard III*—who was played by our own Patrick Taylor—that is designed to raise awareness of domestic violence. We had the first workshop at our annual fundraiser, the proceeds of which go to support Open Windows. Joe donated about $500 worth of bar supplies and alcohol for the event.

You always know where you stand with Joe. At least once a week, he will look me directly in the eye and say, "Thank you." He treats all his employees with respect and that makes it easy to work for him.

~Marianne Riera

AT FIRST WE TRIED HIRING
wait staff in the traditional way,
but the people who responded
didn't have the family spirit that
we wanted to build here. Then late
one night, I think it was actually
about four or five o'clock in the
morning, I thought, *I should just
send out a tweet and see what
happens*. By morning, the resumes
were flooding in. People from all
over the world replied. They were
all Little Monsters. We met with
all the ones who lived in New York
City. Only one had actual restaurant
experience; the rest were just really
good kids that wanted to work at
Joanne because of the connection
to my daughter. So we trained them.
Of the five we hired from that tweet,
three are still here. The ones who
left us had to move on, but they still
come back from time to time and
when they need work they'll pick up
a few shifts here and there.

Alex, one of the waiters, is
Natali's boyfriend. They met at
Parsons School of Design and
have been together for years. He's
a photographer and is very good
with computers, so I've hired him
to deal with all the social media for
the restaurant. Emily is a talented
graphic designer. She does the party
and catering menus. Mikey was with
us from the beginning, but he has
since moved on to pursue his career
as a performer. He's an incredibly

Cynthia's birthday dinner, 2015. (Back row from left to right: Joe and Fran Maniscalco, Cynthia and Joe Germanotta. Front row: Alex Dolan and Natali Germanotta).

talented artist and we keep his
drawing of the restaurant on the
wall. Elise is a writer. She wrote a
beautiful poem about the restaurant that we put up on our website.
Virginia shares Stefani's love of the
nightlife and culture of the Lower
East Side. In one of those odd twists
of fate, after she started working
here she began dating a musician
who turned out to be an old friend of
Stefani's from her days living down
on Stanton Street. Marianne is a
theater activist whose work raises
awareness for victims of domestic

violence. Patrick, Josh, and Laura
run a theater company called Dark
Matter Productions. Laura actually
came in to interview as bartender.
She still picks up shifts whenever
we need help at the restaurant, but
from the moment we met I knew
there was something special about
her so I hired her to work for me as
my assistant.

All the staff, from the kitchen to
the front of house, are team players.
They help each other out because
we are a family.

~*Joe Germanotta*

DON'T LET MY DAD FOOL YOU; he is an artist. There's a drawing that used to hang in my grandparents' house, it was at the foot of the stairs on the second landing. It was a beautiful line drawing of Big Ben in black ink on parchment. The detail was amazing. I had seen it my whole life and then one day I asked my grandmother about it and she told me it was my father's. I had no idea he could draw like that.

I get my love of fashion from my grandmother. She made all our baby clothes. One of my favorites that she made for me was a faux fur outfit with a matching faux fur muff. We have a lot of sweaters that my Aunt Joanne knitted. Both my sister and I used to wear them all the time. I never got to meet Joanne, but I feel very connected to her from sharing stories with my grandma and my dad. Everyone says I look just like her and talk just like her.

~Natali Germanotta

I GREW UP IN HUNTINGTON, West Virginia, about two hours south of Cynthia's hometown; her brother, Doug, and I both went to Marshall University. I always knew I would end up in New York and Joanne was my very first job in the city. I had applied in response to one of Joe's tweets, but I wasn't living in the city at the time so they didn't call me in. I didn't hear anything for months and then one day I got an email from Ana out of the blue. She was slammed and needed help behind the bar. I started working in November 2013 and then I immediately booked an acting job in Ohio that December. I was nervous to tell Joe because most restaurants will fill your position if you book an acting gig out of town, but he totally understood. He said to me, "I know how the business works, you'll have a place here when you come back."

My craziest day at Joanne was Father's Day 2015. Cynthia's family was in town and all her West Virginia people were having Sunday brunch out on the patio. Tony Bennett's family was at the Chef's Table and there was a big group from Stefani's tour in the main dining room. It was just me, Emily and Elise working that day and we were running back and forth between the three parties, helping one another out. Stefani ended up hopping behind the bar, making wine spritzers for everybody; there were bottles everywhere and limes strewn all over the bar. I was bartending that night, so of course I was keeping a watchful eye.

~Josh Meredith

Natali and Stefani.

Stefani, Joe, and Natali.

Top: *Natali and Stefani with their grandfather, Joseph Anthony Germanotta.* Bottom: *Natali and Stefani with their grandparents, Angelina and Joseph Germanotta.*

Stefani (age 2) feeding Cynthia.

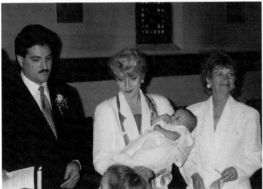

The Germanotta and Bissett families at Natali's christening.

Bissett family (from left to right: Paul Bissett, Cynthia, Natali, Stefani, and Ronnie Bissett).

Natali with grandparents, Paul Douglas Bissett and Veronica Rose "Ronnie" Bissett.

Joe and Stefani present their homemade "pumpkin" cake for the holiday.

Germanotta and Benedetto Family Portrait (from left to right: Cynthia Germanotta, Susan Benedetto, Tony Bennett, Lady Gaga, Natali Germanotta, Joe Germanotta, and Danny Bennett).

Stefani and Joe.

Joe, taking down the old awning at 70 West 68th Street.

Joe and Cynthia in Venice.

(Above) Natali throwing coins in Trevi Fountain. (Right) Joe and Natali in Rome.

Joe and Cynthia in front of the fireplace at Joanne during the holidays.

The Germanottas pick out and bring home a Christmas tree every year. (From left to right: Joe, Stefani, Cynthia, and Natali).

Joe at the Piazza San Marco on a family trip to Venice in 2001.

Joe and Cynthia at the Ampeleia Vineyard in Tuscany.

Making fresh, homemade marinara in the Maniscalco's backyard.

Papa G slicing potatoes for the annual late August marinara-making feast with the Maniscalcos.

Joe, Natali, and Cynthia on horseback at Black Mountain Ranch in Colorado.

Cynthia, Stefani, and Angelina Germanotta.

Joe and Cynthia.

Stefani with Grandpa Paul and Grandma Ronnie eating a big Italian dinner at the Bissett family table in West Virginia.

Natali with Grandpa Joseph Germanotta. Joseph's antique clock (background) now adorns the mantle above the wood-burning fireplace at Joanne.

Natali and Stefani (ages 10 and 16)—Natali is wearing the Mother Seton School sweatshirt that used to belong to Joanne.

Stefani and Cynthia sharing gelato at the restaurant, before it became Joanne Trattoria.

Stefani and Cynthia.

Joe and Stefani.

Chapter 6

Desserts

When I was little I was always super eager to help my dad cook. For the holidays we always went to my grandparents' house in New Jersey. We would start prepping the night before; my dad would make the whole meal and be very grumpy. It was always my grandmother who helped my dad cook; my mom and I are the bakers in our family. We started off slow, making a pumpkin pie on Thanksgiving. Then we added apple and pecan pies.

I love to bake, but over the years I've had my fair share of disasters. One year, I got really ambitious and I sliced all the apples for my pies too early. Of course, they all turned brown and I was mortified. To cover my mistake, I tossed them all in a saucepan with some brown sugar. I was just like, *roll with it.* I made my crust and popped the pies in the oven and when they were done I left them to cool near the window. I was just so relieved that they were done and no one was the wiser about my brown apples. Then, I heard my dad screaming, "No, Alice!" Our dog had eaten half of each one of my pies. She was so full, she spent the rest of the night sacked out on living room floor.

Another time, I had seen on a cooking show a coconut cake in the shape of a bunny. I thought this would be great for Easter, so I painstakingly make these bunny cakes with coconut fur and jelly bean eyes. I put them in the fridge to cool and when I went to pull them out the whole tray slid on the floor and the cakes were destroyed. I've learned to be much more careful when baking.

Natali with Alice, the pie eater.

My mom and Merle Green Steinberg have been close friends for years; she's known her longer than she's known my dad. Over the years, we've spent a lot of family time with Merle and her husband Bob (who has now passed away) and we always referred to them as "Aunt Merle and Uncle Bobby." When we were growing up we spent summers together in the Hamptons, and got together for the holidays. I have so many fond memories of our two families cooking together and having fun. Aunt Merle taught me how to make my favorite dessert: Yogurt Pie. You layer low-fat yogurt and Cool Whip with dark chocolate chips in a graham cracker piecrust. Stick it in the freezer for a couple of hour and serve cold.

~Natali Germanotta

Pizzelle

These thin, crisp waffle cookies are traditionally made at Christmas and Easter. The name comes from the Italian word for "round" or "flat" (the word pizza *has the same origin).*

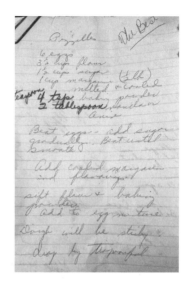

Makes: About 60 pizzelle

Ingredients

6 eggs

3½ cups flour

1½ cups sugar

1 cup margarine (½ lb.), melted and cooled

4 tsp. baking powder

2 tbsp. vanilla or anise extract

Pizzelle iron

1. In a medium bowl, beat eggs.
2. Gradually stir in sugar and beat until smooth.
3. Add cooled margarine and vanilla.
4. Sift flour and baking powder and add to egg mixture. Blend until smooth.
5. Drop the batter mixture one teaspoon at a time onto the pizzelle iron.
6. Bake according to the pizelle iron specifications, usually between 20 and 45 seconds.
7. Carefully remove cookies from the pizelle iron and allow to cool completely before storing in an airtight container.

Nutellasagna

Travis Jones's Nutellasagna is our most popular dessert. What kid—
or adult for that matter—can resist layer upon layer of crisp puff pastry,
creamy mascarpone and, of course, warm melt-in-your-mouth Nutella?

Serves: 8–12

Ingredients

16 oz. mascarpone cheese
7 sheets of puff pastry
8 egg yolks, separated into 2 bowls
24 oz. Nutella
1 cup confectioners sugar
3 tbsp. water

1. Preheat oven to 425 degrees.
2. Line a sheet pan with a piece of parchment paper.
3. In a separate bowl mix 3 egg yolks and water to make egg wash for puff pastry and set aside. (3 yolks to 3 tbsp. water.)
4. In an electric mixer with paddle attachment, mix together the mascarpone cheese, the other 5 egg yolks and confectioners sugar until combined and thickened. Set aside.
5. Brush the outside edges of the puff pastry with the egg wash, being careful not to put too much.
6. Take a scoop of Nutella and spread it on the puff pastry evenly, being careful not to get any along the egg-washed edges.
7. Carefully place another piece of puff pastry on top, lining up the edges. On this layer you will do the same and brush egg wash around the edges of the puff pastry.
8. Then take a scoop of mascarpone mixture and spread evenly, careful not to get it on the egg-washed edges.

9. Repeat, alternating between egg-washed layers, mascarpone, and Nutella, until the topmost layer is just the puff pastry.
10. Press down the edges to make sure it's sealed all the way around and that there is no leaking mascarpone. Brush the top with egg wash and place in the oven for 25–35 minutes until the pastry has puffed up and turned golden brown.
11. Serve hot and dust with powdered sugar.

Tiramisu

This classic Italian dessert is made from ladyfingers drenched in coffee liquor and layered with whipped mascarpone, egg yolk, and confectioner's sugar. Serve chilled and lightly dusted with sweetened cocoa powder.

Serves: 4

Ingredients
12 lady fingers
16 oz. mascarpone cheese
6 egg yolks, pasteurized
1 cup confectioners sugar
8 oz. espresso
8 oz. coffee liquor (Kahlua)
8 oz. sweetened cocoa powder

1. Break six ladyfingers into even halves (so you have 12 pieces).
2. In the bottom of an 8 x 8-inch square pan, layer half the lady-fingers pieces (6 halves).
3. Pour 4 oz. of espresso and 4 oz. of coffee liquor onto the lady-fingers and allow them to soak up the mixture.
4. In a mixer with the paddle attachment mix together the mascarpone cheese, confectioners sugar and egg yolks until smooth and slightly thickened.
5. Add half the mascarpone mixture to the pan to cover the layer of ladyfingers.
6. On top of the mascarpone mixture break the remaining ladyfingers in half and repeat the first step again making sure to soak the ladyfingers in the remaining espresso and liquor mixture.
7. For the top, spread the last scoop of mascarpone evenly over the entire pan and lightly dust the top with sweetened cocoa powder and chill.

Sicilian Ricotta Cheesecake

For this recipe you will need a ricotta cheese that is specifically for pastries, so it is not as grainy—you can use regular ricotta, but the texture will be different. It is also best to use a springform pan (used for cheesecakes) because once the ingredients puff up it allows you to remove the sides without damaging the cake.

Servings: 8

Ingredients

4½ lbs. Ricotta Sopraffina

9 eggs

3 tbsp. cinnamon

3 tbsp. orange extract

2 tbsp. vanilla extract

1½ cups granulated sugar

1. Preheat oven to 325 degrees.
2. Spray a 10-inch springform pan with nonstick spray and sprinkle sugar inside to coat the pan thoroughly, tapping out excess.
3. In a mixing bowl combine all ingredients thoroughly and pour into the springform pan. Take a larger pan and place the springform pan inside of it, filling the outer pan with water until it reaches the top. (This creates a water-bath, and allows the cheesecake to cook evenly and makes it more custard-like.)
4. Bake for 35 to 45 min or until golden brown and slightly jiggly. (Use caution when removing the cheesecake from the water bath as the water will be extremely hot and can burn you very easily.)
5. Chill and serve.

Flourless Chocolate Cake

Made with chocolate and cocoa, this dense, rich cake is a chocolate lovers delight. Serve warm with a generous scoop of gelato.

Servings: 8

Ingredients

8 oz. bittersweet chocolate, chopped up

1 cup butter

1½ cups granulated sugar

6 eggs

1 cup cocoa powder

1. Preheat the oven to 350 degrees.
2. Line an 8-inch round or square cake pan with parchment paper and nonstick spray. In a double boiler pot (or place a bowl in a skillet with a couple inches of water), heat butter and chocolate until fully melted and combined.
3. Add sugar and cocoa powder and stir until no lumps are present.
4. Carefully remove the bowl from the skillet and add eggs one at a time; mix well so the eggs do not cook separately.
5. Once fully combined, pour batter into cake pan and place in oven and bake 30 to 45 minutes, until center is firm.

A young Natali bakes a birthday cake for Cynthia.

Remembrances & Musings

JOE AND STEFANI LOVE TO cook, but Natali and I are the bakers in the family. My mother taught me how to make fresh pies with homemade crust when I was a young girl and I passed those recipes, and my love of baking, down to Natali. There was a time when she and I would bake a different pie every month. We also baked cakes, and made cookies and homemade fudge. We even made candy. My father, Paul Bissett, had a wonderful taffy recipe and we had an annual tradition where the whole family would get together for a taffy pull. My father passed away on Easter 2013, but this tradition lives on through his grandchildren who have taken up the taffy-pulling mantel. Joe's mother taught the girls how to make traditional Italian cookies. One of their favorite kinds are pizzelle. Angelina had a special iron and she and the girls would make pizzelle by the hundreds. Joe's father had these tall tins that were the perfect size for storing them.

~Cynthia Germanotta

I COME FROM A LONG LINE OF bakers and excellent cooks on both sides of my family. My Aunt Marilyn is famous back home for her baking and has passed down her recipe for piecrust and croissant rolls to me, which I often use at Joanne. Before my Grandma Vie passed away I was able to get a few recipes of hers that I grew up eating and loving, like her pumpkin pie and her jams and jellies. I love making people happy and that's easy to do when your recipes come from the heart.

If it wasn't for my family teaching me their craft and how to be a good person, which was the most important lesson, I wouldn't be where I am today. I'm just a small town boy from Licking, Missouri. I ask myself every morning, "How did I end up in New York City?"

~Travis Jones

Travis Jones with Aunt Marilyn.

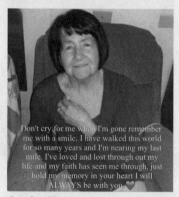

Don't cry for me when I'm gone remember me with a smile, I have walked this world for so many years and I'm nearing my last mile. I've loved and lost through out my life and my faith has seen me through, just hold my memory in your heart I will ALWAYS be with you ♥

Grandma Vie.

FANS FROM ALL OVER THE world come to visit us at the restaurant. One of the most memorable experiences is the time this huge white tour bus pulled up in front of the restaurant. An interpreter came in and asked if they could have lunch. We said, "Of course," and some sixty-plus Japanese tourists filed in. The interpreter spent the rest of the afternoon following the waiter around while he took all their orders.

A lot of fans drop off gifts for Stefani at the restaurant. Most of it is artwork—portraits of her— and some of them are spectacular. One fan did a portrait of her that was made entirely out of beads. We'll put them up on the wall for a while and then I'll send them to the Archives, a 30,000 square-foot storage space where we keep all the outfits and costumes from Stefani's tours and appearances.

Chef Art's husband, Jesus Salgueiro, has done a series of Gaga-inspired, hand-painted dinner plates. They are absolutely stunning. Each one depicts a different one of her looks.

~*Joe Germanotta*

I STARTED AS A BARTENDER, but ended up becoming Mr. G's assistant. I had graduated in 2014 with a BA in Theater, and that summer I began bartending. When I moved to New York a friend of mine worked at Joanne, so I sent my resume to the General manager's email; within ten minutes, Mr. G called me. He asked me to come in that day and work a shift behind the bar. I worked Thursday, Friday, and Saturday as a bar-back. On the Saturday night Mr. and Mrs. G came in for dinner and sat at the table right in front of the bar. I remember I was so nervous, he asked for olive oil and I brought it in the wrong kind of dish.

That January, New York City was hit by a huge snowstorm. I was at dinner with friends and my cell phone rang. Mr. G said, "Laura I need to talk to you," and asked me to come speak to them at their house. The following morning I trudged through a foot of snow to the Germanottas' condo on the Upper West Side. I remember sitting in the living room, Cynthia was curled on a chair and Mr. G was blowing up a medicine ball. I figured he wasn't going to fire me—only a crazy person would invite you to their house if they were going to fire you—but the last thing I expected was for them to offer me a job as Mr. G's personal assistant. I came in the following Monday, they gave me keys to their home, and then they left for the *Oscars*.

I started off my first day feeling pretty confident. I was thinking, *I am so blessed. I just moved to New York and I've got two jobs!* Then I left presents for Elton John's children in the back of a cab. When I got back to their condo, I took off my slushy boots, so I wouldn't get their floors dirty, and promptly slipped in my socks down twelve steps on their circular stairs. After that, I went into Mr. G's office and cried. Then Natali called to ask me to let her into the restaurant. I figured I could at least do that without messing up, but I wound up setting off the alarm just as a police car was driving by.

When Mr. G called later that day, I thought he was going to yell at me for screwing up so badly, but he said, "I heard you fell down the stairs and wanted to know if you're okay." Mrs. G was like "Oh, honey I can tell you're having a bad day." When she got back to town, she bought me a pair of rubber-bottom slippers to wear around the house so I wouldn't slip down the stairs again.

~*Laura Wilson*

He's always been super generous. He sent a bunch of us to the album launch party for *Artpop*. He is at the restaurant every day, making sure everything is running smoothly. If something breaks down or there's a technical issue, Joe takes care of it. Sometimes it's little things, like one time I forgot to tie my hair back before my shift and it kept getting in my eyes. He noticed it was bugging me so he went out and bought me hair ties. I always tell my customers, "Joe is like my second dad."

~Elise Nagel

I STARTED WORKING AT JOANNE in September 2013, but I feel like I've been here my whole life. I got the job through a tweet from Joe. I sent him a one-sentence email in reply. Early the next morning, my cell phone rang. It was a Saturday; I was sleeping and woke up very groggy to this deep, paternal voice, "Hi, this is Joe Germanotta. Can you come and trail at the restaurant tonight?" When I got there that night, he was like, "You look normal." I was a nanny with no restaurant experience, but he hired me on the spot.

I'm usually here even when I'm not working. I used to be a little bit afraid of Joe, but now I'm not. I call him dad—but not to his face.

I REMEMBER JOE CALLED ME while I was in class, taking a Graphic Design History exam. He just kept calling and my cell phone kept ringing and ringing. I finally had to excuse myself and leave the room to answer the call in the hallway. I went in to the restaurant the next day and met Travis and Joe. When he saw on my resume that I had worked in a bakery, he joked that I would give Travis a run for his money. For my day job, I'm a freelance graphic designer. Because Joe is so supportive of the arts, there are a lot of creative people working at Joanne. We all have side projects and I've had the opportunity to collaborate with so many different people.

At Joanne we get a mix of regulars, Lady Gaga fans, and tourists looking for a good place to eat. It's definitely a unique serving experience. Every day, we get the same round of questions. *How many times does Lady Gaga come in? Have you met her? Is she nice?* They always want to know where she sits. Fans call the restaurant from all over the world to chat and ask us about Gaga. We also get a lot of packages and letters for Stefani. Once this huge package arrived and it was a custom-made, Lady Gaga guitar. Another fan painted a David Bowie portrait of her. My favorite was this one letter that was just a list of forty-nine different sandwich recipes, I guess to give us options.

~Emily Villanova

I DO FREELANCE PHOTOGRAPHY and have helped produce a few short videos. In November 2015, I went to Haiti as a photographer with Parsons alum Donna Karan and the Born This Way Foundation. I started working at Joanne about six months after they opened. This place is like a Mecca for Gaga fans. People will come in and tell us their life stories; they'll cry because she's changed their lives.

People will always come in and declare themselves her biggest fan. But arguably her biggest fan is Debbie from Westchester. She always wears her Gaga T-shirt every time she comes to the restaurant. She has a list of stats for how many times she's met Joe, Cynthia, Natali, and of course, Gaga. Her wall is covered in Gaga memorabilia.

~Alex Dolan

I DIDN'T GET THE JOB VIA tweet. I did it the old fashioned way, by dropping off my resume at the restaurant. When I started, Joe welcomed me to the team. I have worked at Joanne for three years, and look forward to many more. It has become my second home.

The Germanottas are very generous people and treat all the staff like we are part of the family. At one point, my foot was swollen and I was having trouble walking. Joe paid for me to go to his podiatrist. It turned out I had a stress fracture. I am very grateful that he helped me out because I probably would have continued working on it and doing even more damage to my foot.

~Virginia Bodenmiller

Chapter 7

Cocktails

I first met Dallas Mayr and Michael Greer at The Aegean, a Greek restaurant on the Upper West Side. We quickly fell into a routine of meeting up in the afternoons after work and got to be friendly with the managers and the bartenders. We liked The Aegean because it was on the corner and the bar had windows facing the street, so we could watch all the people walking by. We started out as a trio, but as the years went by our number grew to about ten or twelve.

When The Aegean closed down, we suddenly found ourselves homeless. We spent some time wandering, searching for the right place to settle back into. We tried a Mexican restaurant for a while, but then that closed down, too. After that, there was a burger place and then a couple of other neighborhood restaurants, but either they weren't the right fit or they would end up closing down. Then one day, I stumbled upon 70 West 68th Street and I knew I had found our new home.

A lot of that had to do with Ana Coste, who is an amazing presence behind the bar. She has this way of making you feel welcome the moment you walk in. When we decided to take over the space and open Joanne, there was never any question that she would stay on with us.

~Joe Germanotta

The Cynthia (Grapefruitini)

Ingredients

½ shaker Hendrick's Gin

Splash of St. Germain

2 oz. grapefruit juice

1. In a bar shaker add all 3 ingredients.

2. Shake well.

3. Pour into a chilled martini glass.

3-Nut Cappuccino

Ingredients
¾ oz. Frangelico
¾ oz. Nocello
¾ oz. Amaretto
8 oz. Cappuccino
Steamed milk

1. In a large cappuccino or coffee cup, pour a shot of espresso.
2. Add the 3 liquors and top with steamed milk and foam.

The Monster

Ingredients
½ shaker Mandarin Vodka
2 oz. pineapple juice
splash of grenadine

1. In a bar shaker with ice, combine ingredients.
2. Shake well and pour into a chilled martini glass.
3. Garnish with an orange slice and maraschino cherry.

Little Monster Mocktail

This light and refreshing virgin martini is a great signature drink for parties and goes great with brunch. You can add either Prosecco or vodka and make the adult version!

Ingredients

2 oz. fresh orange juice
4 oz. fresh pineapple juice
2 oz. apple juice
2 splashes grenadine

1. Fill a bar shaker ⅔ of the way full with ice.
2. Add the orange juice, pineapple juice and apple juice.
3. Put the lid on and shake to mix thoroughly and make it ice cold. Pour into chilled 8 oz. martini glass.
4. Top with two splashes of grenadine for color and garnish with an orange slice on the rim.

Emily Villanova's rendering of Lady Gaga's Joanne *album cover on the chalkboard at the restaurant.*

Remembrances & Musings

I WORKED FOR THE PRIOR owners from 1996, until they closed down in 2011. I was manager and worked behind the bar. I stayed for all those years because of my regulars. Dallas Mayr is the horror/suspense writer Jack Ketchum. Stephen King calls him the "Scariest Man in America." He's lived in the neighborhood forever. He always comes in at five o'clock on the dot and has a Dewar's on the rocks. Alan Goldberg was a producer at *ABC News*. He lives next-door and comes in every night to watch *Jeopardy*. He likes to start the night with a white wine and soda, but he calls it a "Schwarzenegger," so it sounds a bit more macho when he orders it. Michael Greer passed away ten years ago. He died of cancer very quickly. He came in one day to tell us he was sick and then he went into the hospital. Two weeks later he passed away.

In early March of 2011, I got a call from a neighbor that the city marshal had locked the door. Just like that, after fifteen years, I was out of a job. A few days later, Joe called a meeting of all the regulars to discuss what to do next. He said

to me, "Listen kid, don't worry. We're going to take care of you." Soon after, he announced that he and Cynthia were planning to take over the space and open their own restaurant. He gave me my old job back, and he gave back a second home to all the regulars who had been coming here for more than a decade. That's the kind of man Joe is. He takes care of people. That's not to say that he's a pushover; he can be intimidating.

Stefani is so sweet. She loves to go behind the bar and make drinks. Of course, whenever she comes in it's always slammed because word gets out that Lady Gaga is mixing drinks. She'll be back there with her huge heals. She sure is messy, but she's actually a pretty good bartender. Natali is a sweetheart, too. She worked here behind the bar for a while. She's very loving, maternal, and affectionate. And I adore Cynthia; she's been like a mother to me. When we first opened she would stay and help me clean and close out the register.

~Ana Coste

Cynthia Germanotta, Ana Coste, and Kathy McGinty.

I MOVED IN NEXT DOOR TO 70 West 68th Street in 1973. I was convinced it would be temporary, but more than forty years later I'm still next door. In 1989, it became an Italian restaurant. The first time I came in for a drink there was an Irish bartender with a ponytail working behind the bar. He was talking to a woman who was in tears. She was sobbing to him, "What am I going to do when you leave?" Later that night, he quietly explained that it was his last shift behind the bar, but that he had never met the woman before that night.

All the customers seemed like they were directly out of *Goodfellas*. I used to joke with the owner, "If I get whacked in this place, I'm not going to be happy about it." Back then I was working on a documentary about Richard Nixon. The owner was telling some guy at the bar about it and the guy leaned over and said to me, "I'm not wired. You're not wired. What do you really think of Nixon?" It was that kind of place.

I remember when Joe told me, "My daughter, Stefani, is doing music." He played us some of her songs, and we were like, "Oh, this is nice." We had no idea she would go on to become such a big star.

~*Alan Goldberg*

JOSH MEREDITH AND I HAVE been working at Joanne on and off for a few years. We founded a theater company together called Dark Matter. Our focus is theater for social change. Laura, Joe's assistant, is our Co-Marketing and Advocacy Coordinator. When our company put on its first full-length production last fall, both Joe and Cynthia tweeted to their followers that they were coming to the show and told everyone to come "see some of our Joanne family members" if they were in New York. We were all so touched to have their support. Natali and a lot of the Joanne staff (like Emily and Elise) came out to support us as well.

I originally took Josh's job at Joanne when he went off to do summer stock. We'll take a break from working here when there's a production going on but we always come back between shows and Joe will welcome us with open arms. It's like a family. I remember Father's Day 2015, Josh was bartending when Stefani was at the restaurant. The place was crazy packed. Typically, if you have a busy night you'll have a bartender and a bar-back to assist and he or she will get a portion of the bartender's tips, it's called *tipping out*. So the bar was packed and Stefani's back there making drinks and, towards the end of the night, Josh joked to her, "I'll tip you out" and she said, with all sincerity, "No, no. Don't tip me out." We were laughing because here she is Lady Gaga, an international superstar, and she was worried that Josh was really going to give her a portion of his tips.

~*Patrick Taylor*

I MET JOE FIFTEEN YEARS AGO. I was sitting alone at the bar of The Aegean and we struck up a conversation. From that night on, we began meeting regularly for a drink in the evenings after work. I had met Michael Greer five years earlier. He was a composer and lyricist. At some point he had injured his vocal cords, so his voice had become gravely. He was a quiet guy and he always sat at the bar with a yellow notepad. If I tried to talk to him while he was writing, he'd say, "Shut up, Dallas." He had that damned notepad with him all the time. By the time The Aegean closed down, the three of us had bonded enough to go out in search of a new home.

We began scanning the neighborhood for a new place. We would carry around an entourage from bar to bar and when one closed down we would have to find another. There was a whole group of us. It was an eclectic mix of people. We were day laborers, artists, writers, actors, singers. One guy was a teacher at Hunter College, another woman was a book publisher. We used to joke that we were the Angels of Death because no sooner had we settled into a new place it would end up closing down.

Joe was the one who found us 70 W. 68th Street. The bar area was very small, just eight or ten stools. Normally I like a bigger bar—I never sit because if you don't like

who you're talking to you can move on—but Ana made us feel right at home. We brought in a dozen regulars with us. We would come in every day after work around five o'clock. That's when we met Alan, who lives next door. He came in every night at seven o'clock to watch *Jeopardy*.

~Dallas Mayr

70 WEST 68TH STREET IS A landmark building. It was built in the late 1800s. When I worked for the previous owner I got to know the woman who grew up here and she told me stories of how the place used to look. The patio was a backyard where she used to play when she was a young girl in the early 1900s. There used to be a hundred-year-old tree back there, but it got sick and the previous owners had it cut down.

We have our very own ghost at Joanne. I call him Gulpy. Once I was telling a customer the story of how, at some point, maybe forty years ago, when it was liquor store, a Dominican kid had tried to rob the place. The manager shot and killed him where the bar is now. I was telling the guy how the front door will open and shut, glasses will go flying off the wall, doors will lock from the inside, and the lights will shut off on us. He laughed and told

me I was crazy. Suddenly, I saw him duck as one of the martini shakers from the shelf on the wall behind the bar went flying at his head. He said, "I'm getting the hell out of here," and I called after him, "Do you believe me now?"

Over the years we've brought in a priest to bless the restaurant. I even had a friend who sits on the Native American council of advisors come in to sage the place. When she went down to the basement where we have our second kitchen and storage, there was a lot of smoke activity—supposedly if there's a spirit it causes the sage to

really smoke up. All of a sudden we heard a loud boom, like somebody kicked a bucket. Travis screamed and nearly jumped in her arms. When things like that happen I'll shout, "Stop it, Gulpy. I'm not in the mood." I started calling him Gulpy after I began leaving shots of liquor out for him because that seemed to calm him down.

Once Stefani's bodyguard was sitting at the bar having a Pellegrino and Spaghetti Bolognese. I was opening a bottle of wine when something pushed into him and he went flying backwards. It was a force coming from behind the bar, almost

like a gunshot. He's a huge guy, so it must have been incredibly strong to knock him off his stool. Later that same day, Stefani came in with her assistant. As they were walking past the bar, something went *whoosh* and pushed her assistant into the table. I said, "That is not nice, Gulpy. These are good people." Then this guy came and sat down at the table next to the bar. He wasn't very nice, so I said, "Gulpy, why don't you push *him*?" As the guy was leaving, he went flying into the wall. Thank you Gulpy!

~Ana Coste

PAINTER NEAL MCPHEETERS was a member of our group. I walked in one day and he was scribbling on a cocktail napkin. When I approached him, he shushed me and went back to his scribbling. After a while, he handed me the napkin and said, "I want you to write this." It was a little vignette about a kid in the Depression who refuses to eat. I sat on it for years until one day I decided to pick up the story. It ended up becoming the basis for "The Box," which is my most reprinted story.

I've known Stefani since she was a teenager. Michael, Joe, and I used to go downtown to watch her perform at piano bars on the Lower East Side. She was living down on Stanton Street back then. When Michael got sick, I went to the hospital to visit him and bring him some airline bottles of scotch. When I walked into his room, there was Stefani sitting at his bedside, rubbing his feet.

~Dallas Mayr

ALAN: "WE ALL LOVE ANA. When I started coming here, she allowed me something bartenders don't normally do, which was to open the bottles of wine."

ANA: "Over the years he got too lazy, though."

IT'S ALWAYS BEEN REALLY incredible to come into the restaurant and chat with these people who have known me my whole life. That's always been my favorite part. When I was in high school, I used to stop in on my way home from school. My dad would be here with Alan and Dallas and all the other regulars. Ana would be behind the bar. It was all these familiar faces and they have all supported and encouraged me my entire life.

After I graduated from Parsons I started working in fashion, so I don't work at the restaurant anymore. But if you ask anyone they still see me at least two times a week. I'll come in on the weekends to have brunch with my mom or to have lunch with Emily and Elise. Or I'll stop in after work to chat with the regulars and watch *Jeopardy* or *Wheel of Fortune* with them at the bar.

We all come here for the same reason: to touch base with a familiar face. Joanne is our second home.

~Natali Germanotta

A TOAST TO JOANNE

Voices heard laughing,
buzzing joyful sounds,
we take pride in our establishment,
it's a home, not just a haus.
"Just like grandma's kitchen,"
with family recipes we make,
excited children walking on,
"did you see that cake?!"
A hearty Joanne greeting
as you enter through the bar,
spotlight on the chef,
he knows you've traveled far.
Jakarta, Berlin, Barcelona, Rio,
we've welcomed many languages,
we've served many people.
You've touched our hearts,
we long to do the same,
we won't forget your face,
we'll remember your name.
We've become a family,
a home away from home,
come join us for dinner,
you'll never feel alone.

~Elise Nagel

For a Moment

Yesterday, I took a walk in the rain
The cool refreshing droplets splashed on my cheeks.
I walked,
And walked, And walked,
Not knowing where I was going.
The trees swayed as a chilly spring
Gently caressed their branches.
A cute white rabbit scampered
Across a wide open field.
He stopped in front of me in a
Patch of emerald.
He had a quizzical look on his furry little face.
He wiggled his ears,
Crinkled his nose,
And scratched his whiskers like
An old man.
I started to laugh.
He ran off into the distance
Looking like a pearl in a patch of seaweed.
The cool refreshing droplets splashed
On my cheeks.

I walked,
And walked, And walked,
Not knowing where I was going.
I saw a family of ducks on a lake,
I stopped to look,
Mama Duck first,
And all the little ducklings gliding
Behind her in a single file.
They were dancing to the music
of the rain tapping on water.
And then I was my reflection on
the mirror-like surface of the lake
And for a moment…
I was the only living creature around.
The cool refreshing droplets splashed
On my cheeks. I turned,
And walked, And walked,
Knowing where I was going.

~*Joanne Germanotta*

Notes

Notes

Notes

Notes